Rich with realistic details, Jessica Boyer's amigurumi are super easy to create with mostly single crochet stitches. Dimensions range from the Puffer Fish at 5 inches long to the Shark at 12 inches.

LEISURE ARTS, INC. • Maumelle, Arkansas

Finished Size: Approximately 5" (12.5 cm) diameter (excluding arms and legs)

CRAB

SHELL

Row 1: With Red, ch 2, 2 sc in second ch from hook.

Row 2: Ch 1, turn; 2 sc in each sc: 4 sc.

Row 3: Ch 1, turn; sc in first sc, 2 sc in next sc, sc in next sc, 2 sc in last sc: 6 sc.

Row 4: Ch 1, turn; sc in first 2 sc, 2 sc in next sc, sc in next 2 sc, 2 sc in last sc: 8 sc.

Row 5: Ch 1, turn; sc in first 3 sc, 2 sc in next sc, sc in next 3 sc, 2 sc in last sc: 10 sc.

Row 6: Ch 1, turn; sc in first 4 sc, 2 sc in next sc, sc in next 4 sc, 2 sc in last sc: 12 sc.

Row 7: Ch 1, turn; sc in first 5 sc, 2 sc in next sc, sc in next 5 sc, 2 sc in last sc: 14 sc.

Begin working in rnds.

Rnd 1 (Right side)**:** Ch 1, turn; sc in first 6 sc, 2 sc in next sc, sc in next 6 sc, 3 sc in last sc; skip first row, sc in end of next 6 rows; 3 sc in free loop of beginning ch *(Fig. 3b, page 46)*; sc in end of next 7 rows; do **not** join, place marker to indicate beginning of rnd *(see Markers, page 45)*: 33 sc.

Note: Loop a short piece of yarn around any sc to mark Rnd 1 as **right** side.

Rnd 2: 3 Sc in next sc, sc in next 14 sc, 3 sc in next sc, sc in next 17 sc: 37 sc.

Rnd 3: Sc in next sc, 2 sc in each of next 2 sc, sc in next 14 sc, 2 sc in each of next 2 sc, sc in next 18 sc: 41 sc.

Rnd 4: (Sc in next sc, 2 sc in next sc) twice, (sc in next 3 sc, 2 sc in next sc) 4 times, sc in next sc, 2 sc in next sc, sc in next 19 sc: 48 sc.

Rnd 5: 2 Sc in next sc, sc in next 3 sc, 2 sc in next sc, (sc in next 4 sc, 2 sc in next sc) 4 times, sc in next 3 sc, 2 sc in next sc, sc in next 19 sc: 55 sc.

Rnd 6: Sc in each sc around.

Rnd 7: Sc in each sc around to last 5 sc; move marker to indicate new beginning of rnd.

Rnd 8: Working in Front Loops Only *(Fig. 2, page 45)*, 3 sc in next sc, (sc in next sc, 3 sc in next sc) twice, sc in next 3 sc, 3 sc in next sc, ★ skip next sc, sc in next sc, skip next sc, 3 sc in next sc; repeat from ★ 5 times **more**, sc in next 3 sc, 3 sc in next sc, (sc in next sc, 3 sc in next sc) twice, sc in next 14 sc; slip st in same st as first sc, finish off.

BODY

Rnd 1: With **right** side facing and working in free loops of Rnd 7 on Shell *(Fig. 3a, page 45)*, skip 4 sc from last sc made and join Tan with sc in next sc *(see Joining With Sc, page 45)*, sc in each sc around; do **not** join, place marker: 55 sc.

Rnd 2: Working in both loops, (sc2tog, sc in next 9 sc) around: 50 sc.

Rnd 3: (Sc2tog, sc in next 8 sc) around: 45 sc.

Rnd 4: (Sc2tog, sc in next 7 sc) around: 40 sc.

Rnd 5: (Sc2tog, sc in next 6 sc) around: 35 sc.

The loop can be slipped from the hook onto a safety pin while attaching the eyes and embroidering the mouth.

Use photos as guides for placement of all pieces and for embroidery. See Tips, page 45.

Attach safety eyes to Rnd 1 of the Body, lined up with curved portion of center of Shell and spacing them approximately 5 sc apart.

With Black, embroider mouth across top of 3 sc on Rnd 2, centered between eyes, using backstitch *(Fig. 6, page 46)*.

Rnd 6: (Sc2tog, sc in next 5 sc) around: 30 sc.

Rnd 7: (Sc2tog, sc in next 4 sc) around: 25 sc.

Rnd 8: (Sc2tog, sc in next 3 sc) around: 20 sc.

Rnd 9: (Sc2tog, sc in next 2 sc) around: 15 sc.

Stuff Body with polyester fiberfill.

Rnd 10: (Sc2tog, sc in next sc) around: 10 sc.

Rnd 11: Sc2tog around: 5 sc.

Continue to sc2tog around until hole is closed; slip st in next sc, finish off.

ARM (Make 2)
UPPER ARM

With Red, ch 3.

Rnd 1 (Right side)**:** Sc in second ch from hook, 3 sc in last ch; 2 sc in free loop of ch at base of first sc; do **not** join, place marker: 6 sc.

Rnd 2: (Sc in next 2 sc, 3 sc in next sc) twice: 10 sc.

Rnds 3-7: Sc in each sc around.

Stuff Upper Arm with polyester fiberfill.

Rnd 8: Sc2tog around; slip st in next sc, finish off leaving a long end for sewing: 5 sc.

Use whipstitch *(Fig. 5, page 46)* for the method of sewing to join the pieces together.

Sew last rnd of Upper Arm to Body.

CLAW
FIRST HALF

Rnd 1 (Right side)**:** With Black, make an adjustable loop to form a ring *(Figs. 1a-d, page 45)*; work 4 sc in ring; do **not** join, place marker.

Rnd 2: Sc in each sc around.

Rnd 3: (Sc in next sc, 2 sc in next sc) twice: 6 sc.

Rnd 4: Sc in each sc around changing to Red in last sc made *(Fig. 4a, page 46)*.

Rnds 5 and 6: Sc in each sc around.

Finish off leaving a long end for sewing.

SECOND HALF

Rnds 1-4: Work same as First Half changing to Tan in last sc made on Rnd 4: 6 sc.

Rnd 5: Sc in each sc around.

5

Rnd 6: Sc in next 5 sc, holding both halves side by side, sc in next 5 sc on First Half: 10 sc.

Sew the 2 unworked sc closed.

Rnd 7: Sc in each sc around changing to Red in last sc made.

Rnds 8-10: Sc in each sc around.

Stuff Claw with polyester fiberfill.

Rnd 11: Sc2tog around; slip st in next sc, finish off leaving a long end for sewing: 5 sc.

Sew Claw to Upper Arm.

LEG (Make 6)
UPPER LEG

Rnd 1 (Right side)**:** With Red, make an adjustable loop to form a ring; work 6 sc in ring; do **not** join, place marker.

Rnds 2-7: Sc in each sc around.

Slip st in next sc, finish off leaving a long end for sewing.

LOWER LEG

Work same as Upper Leg through Rnd 4.

Slip st in next sc, finish off leaving a long end for sewing.

Stuff Upper and Lower Legs firmly with polyester fiberfill.

Sew Lower Leg to Upper Leg at an angle.

Pin the Legs to the Body; sew in place.

SEAHORSE

HEAD

Rnd 1 (Right side)**:** With Yellow, make
an adjustable loop to form a ring
(Figs. 1a-d, page 45); work 6 sc in
ring; do **not** join, place marker to
indicate beginning of rnd *(see
Markers, page 45)*.

Rnd 2: 2 Sc in each sc around: 12 sc.

Rnd 3: (Sc in next sc, 2 sc in next sc)
around: 18 sc.

Rnd 4: (Sc in next 2 sc, 2 sc in next sc)
around: 24 sc.

Rnd 5: (Sc in next 3 sc, 2 sc in next sc)
around: 30 sc.

Rnds 6-11: Sc in each sc around.

The loop can be slipped from
the hook onto a safety pin while
attaching the eyes.

Use photos as guides for placement
of all pieces. See Tips, page 45.

Attach safety eyes to Rnd 8 spacing
them approximately 5 sc apart.

Rnd 12: (Sc2tog, sc in next 3 sc)
around: 24 sc.

Rnd 13: (Sc2tog, sc in next 2 sc)
around: 18 sc.

Stuff Head with polyester fiberfill.

Rnd 14: (Sc2tog, sc in next sc)
around: 12 sc.

Rnd 15: Sc2tog around: 6 sc.

Continue to sc2tog around until hole
is closed; slip st in next sc, finish off.

Eyelid (Make 2)**:** With Yellow, ch 3;
finish off leaving a long end for
sewing.

Sew Eyelids to Head above the safety
eyes.

SNOUT

END (Make 2)
Rnd 1 (Right side)**:** With Yellow, ch 2,
6 sc in second ch from hook; do **not**
join, place marker.

Rnds 2 and 3: Sc in each sc around.

Finish off first End only leaving a long
end for sewing.

BODY

Rnd 1 (Joining)**:** Sc in next 4 sc, sc in next 3 sc on first End, leave remaining sc unworked; do **not** join, move marker for new beginning of rnd: 7 sc.

Sew unworked sc of Ends together.

Rnds 2-5: Sc in each sc around.

Rnd 6: 2 Sc in each sc around; slip st in next sc, finish off leaving a long end for sewing: 14 sc.

Stuff Snout with polyester fiberfill.

Use whipstitch *(Fig. 5, page 46)* for the method of sewing to join the pieces together.

Sew Snout to Head, centering it under the safety eyes; pinch the area between the eyes together to form a bridge and make a couple of stitches from side to side near the inner eyes to hold it in place.

NECK

Work same as Head through Rnd 5: 30 sc.

Rnd 6: Sc in Back Loop Only of each sc around *(Fig. 2, page 45)*.

Rnd 7: Sc in both loops of each sc around.

Rnds 8 and 9: Repeat Rnds 6 and 7.

Rnd 10: Sc in Back Loop Only of each sc around; slip st in next sc, finish off leaving a long end for sewing.

BODY

Rnd 1 (Right side)**:** With Yellow, make an adjustable loop to form a ring; work 6 sc in ring; do **not** join, place marker.

Rnd 2: Working in Back Loops Only, 2 sc in each sc around: 12 sc.

Rnd 3: Working in Back Loops Only, (sc in next sc, 2 sc in next sc) around: 18 sc.

Rnd 4: Working in Back Loops Only, (sc in next 2 sc, 2 sc in next sc) around: 24 sc.

Rnd 5: Working in Back Loops Only, (sc in next 3 sc, 2 sc in next sc) around: 30 sc.

Rnd 6: Sc in Back Loop Only of each sc around.

Rnd 7: Sc in both loops of each sc around.

Rnds 8-21: Repeat Rnds 6 and 7, 7 times.

Rnd 22: Sc in Back Loop Only of each sc around; slip st in next sc, finish off leaving a long end for sewing.

Stuff Neck and Body with polyester fiberfill.

Place Neck over Head at an angle and sew in place. Place Body over Neck at an angle and sew in place.

BELLY

With Yellow, ch 12.

Rnd 1 (Right side)**:** Sc in second ch from hook and in each ch across to last ch, 3 sc in last ch; working in free loops of beginning ch *(Fig. 3b, page 46)*, dc in next 9 chs, 2 sc in next ch; do **not** join, place marker: 24 sc.

Note: Loop a short piece of yarn around any sc to mark Rnd 1 as **right** side.

Rnd 2: ★ 2 Sc in next sc, sc in next 9 sc, 2 sc in next sc, sc in next sc; repeat from ★ once **more**: 28 sc.

Rnd 3: ★ 2 Sc in each of next 2 sc, sc in next 8 sc, 2 sc in each of next 2 sc, sc in next 2 sc; repeat from ★ once **more**: 36 sc.

Rnd 4: Sc in Back Loop Only of each sc around.

Rnd 5: Sc in both loops of each sc around; slip st in next sc, finish off leaving a long end for sewing.

Sew Belly to Body stuffing with polyester fiberfill before closing.

TAIL

Rnd 1 (Right side)**:** With Yellow, make an adjustable loop to form a ring; work 6 sc in ring; do **not** join, place marker.

Rnds 2 and 3: Sc in each sc around.

Rnds 4-6: 2 Sc in each of next 2 sc, sc2tog twice: 6 sc.

Rnds 7 and 8: Sc in each sc around.

Rnds 9-11: Sc2tog, 2 sc in each of next 2 sc, sc2tog: 6 sc.

Rnds 12 and 13: Sc in each sc around.

Rnd 14: (Sc in next 2 sc, 2 sc in next sc) twice: 8 sc.

Rnds 15-17: Sc in next sc, sc2tog twice, sc in next sc, 2 sc in each of next 2 sc: 8 sc.

Rnd 18: (Sc in next sc, 2 sc in next sc) around: 12 sc.

Rnds 19 and 20: Sc in each sc around.

Rnd 21: (Sc in next sc, 2 sc in next sc) around: 18 sc.

Rnd 22: Sc in Back Loop Only of each sc around.

Rnd 23: Sc in both loops of each sc around; slip st in next sc, finish off leaving a long end for sewing.

Stuff Tail with polyester fiberfill.

Sew Tail to Body; curl end of Tail and tack in place.

FINS
PECTORAL FIN (Make 2)
Row 1: With Gold, ch 4, dc in fourth ch from hook, (ch 1, dc) twice in same ch; finish off leaving a long end for sewing.

Sew Pectoral Fins to side of Head.

UPPER BACK FIN
With Gold, ch 28.

Row 1: 2 Sc in second ch from hook, skip next ch, sc in next ch, ★ skip next ch, 5 dc in next ch, skip next ch, sc in next ch; repeat from ★ 5 times **more**; finish off leaving a long end for sewing.

Sew Upper Back Fin across Head, Neck, and Body.

DORSAL FIN
Row 1: With Gold, ch 5, tr in fifth ch from hook, (ch 1, tr in same ch) 4 times; finish off leaving a long end for sewing.

Sew Dorsal Fin to center of Body.

LOWER BACK FIN
With Gold, ch 28.

Row 1: 3 Sc in second ch from hook, (skip next ch, sc in next ch, skip next ch, 3 sc in next ch) twice, (skip next ch, sc in next ch, skip next ch, 3 dc in next ch) 3 times, skip next ch, sc in next ch, skip next ch, 3 hdc in next ch, skip next ch, sc in last ch; finish off leaving a long end for sewing.

Sew Lower Back Fin across Tail and lower part of Body.

Finished Size: Approximately 8" diameter x 3½" high (20.5 cm x 9 cm)

HEAD

Rnd 1 (Right side)**:** With Dark Orange, make an adjustable loop to form a ring *(Figs. 1a-d, page 45)*; work 6 sc in ring; do **not** join, place marker to indicate beginning of rnd *(see Markers, page 45)*.

Rnd 2: 2 Sc in each sc around: 12 sc.

Rnd 3: (Sc in next sc, 2 sc in next sc) around: 18 sc.

Rnd 4: (Sc in next 2 sc, 2 sc in next sc) around: 24 sc.

Rnd 5: (Sc in next 3 sc, 2 sc in next sc) around: 30 sc.

Rnd 6: (Sc in next 4 sc, 2 sc in next sc) around: 36 sc.

Rnd 7: (Sc in next 5 sc, 2 sc in next sc) around: 42 sc.

Rnd 8: (Sc in next 6 sc, 2 sc in next sc) around: 48 sc.

Rnds 9-14: Sc in each sc around.

Rnd 15: (Sc in next 7 sc, 2 sc in next sc) around: 54 sc.

The loop can be slipped from the hook onto a safety pin while embroidering the mouth.

Use photos as guides for embroidery and placement of all pieces. See Tips, page 45.

With Black, embroider mouth on Rnd 12, using backstitch *(Fig. 6, page 46)*.

Rnds 16 and 17: Sc in each sc around.

Rnd 18: Sc in each sc around changing to Orange in last sc made *(Fig. 4a, page 46)*.

Rnd 19: Working in Back Loops Only *(Fig. 2, page 45)*, (sc2tog, sc in next 7 sc) around: 48 sc.

Rnd 20: Working in both loops, (sc2tog, sc in next 6 sc) around: 42 sc.

Rnd 21: (Sc2tog, sc in next 5 sc) around: 36 sc.

Rnd 22: (Sc2tog, sc in next 4 sc) around: 30 sc.

Rnd 23: (Sc2tog, sc in next 3 sc) around: 24 sc.

Rnd 24: (Sc2tog, sc in next 2 sc) around: 18 sc.

Stuff Head with polyester fiberfill.

Rnd 25: (Sc2tog, sc in next sc) around: 12 sc.

Rnd 26: Sc2tog around: 6 sc.

Continue to sc2tog around until hole is closed; slip st in next sc, finish off.

EYE (Make 2)

Rnd 1 (Right side)**:** With Dark Orange, make an adjustable loop to form a ring; work 6 sc in ring; do **not** join, place marker.

Rnd 2: 2 Sc in each sc around: 12 sc.

Rnd 3: Working in Back Loops Only, sc in next 6 sc, (sc in next sc, 2 sc in next sc) 3 times: 15 sc.

Rnd 4: Sc in both loops of next 6 sc, slip st in next sc, leave remaining 8 sc unworked; finish off leaving a long end for sewing.

Attach safety eyes to center of Eyes.

Use whipstitch *(Fig. 5, page 46)* for the method of sewing to join the pieces together.

Sew each Eye to Head adding a small amount of polyester fiberfill before closing.

ARMS

UPPER ARM (Make 8)

Rnd 1 (Right side): With Dark Orange, make an adjustable loop to form a ring; work 6 sc in ring; do **not** join, place marker.

Rnd 2: 2 Sc in each sc around: 12 sc.

Rnds 3-5: Sc in each sc around.

Rnd 6: (Sc in next sc, 2 sc in next sc) around; slip st in next sc, finish off leaving a long end for sewing: 18 sc.

Stuff Upper Arm with polyester fiberfill.

Pin each Upper Arm to Rnds 14-18 of Head and sew in place.

ARM TIP (Make 8)

Rnd 1 (Right side): With Dark Orange, make an adjustable loop to form a ring; work 6 sc in ring; do **not** join, place marker.

Rnds 2 and 3: Sc in each sc around.

Rnd 4: 2 Sc in each of next 3 sc, sc in next 3 sc: 9 sc.

Rnds 5-7: Sc in each sc around.

Rnd 8: 2 Sc in each of next 6 sc, sc in next 3 sc: 15 sc.

Rnds 9 and 10: Sc in each sc around.

Slip st in next sc, finish off leaving a long end for sewing.

Stuff Arm Tips with polyester fiberfill.

Sew Arm Tips to Upper Arms at a slight angle, pointing up.

UNDERSIDE (Make 8)

With Orange, ch 16.

Rnd 1 (Right side): Dc in third ch from hook and in next 4 chs, hdc in next 5 chs, sc in next 3 chs, 3 sc in last ch; working in free loops of beginning ch *(Fig. 3b, page 46)*, sc in next 3 chs, hdc in next 5 chs, dc in next 6 chs; finish off leaving a long end for sewing.

Sew 13 buttons to **right** side of Underside, **or** embroider circles using Satin Stitch if safety is an issue *(Fig. 8, page 46)*.

Sew Underside to bottom of Arms.

Sew remaining 24 buttons to bottom of Octopus.

Finished Size: Approximately 3½" high x 5" long (9 cm x 12.5 cm)

PUFFER FISH

BODY

Rnd 1 (Right side)**:** With Gold, make an adjustable loop to form a ring (**Figs. 1a-d, page 45**); work 6 sc in ring; do **not** join, place marker to indicate beginning of rnd (**see Markers, page 45**).

Rnd 2: 2 Sc in each sc around: 12 sc.

Rnd 3: (Sc in next sc, 2 sc in next sc) around: 18 sc.

Rnd 4: (Sc in next 2 sc, 2 sc in next sc) around: 24 sc.

Rnd 5: (Sc in next 3 sc, 2 sc in next sc) around: 30 sc.

Rnd 6: (Sc in next 4 sc, 2 sc in next sc) around: 36 sc.

Rnd 7: (Sc in next 5 sc, 2 sc in next sc) around: 42 sc.

Rnd 8: (Sc in next 6 sc, 2 sc in next sc) around: 48 sc.

Rnds 9-12: Sc in each sc around.

Rnd 13: Sc in each sc around changing to Aran in last sc made (**Fig. 4a, page 46**).

Rnds 14-17: Sc in each sc around.

Rnd 18: (Sc2tog, sc in next 6 sc) around: 42 sc.

Rnd 19: (Sc2tog, sc in next 5 sc) around: 36 sc.

The loop can be slipped from the hook onto a safety pin while attaching the eyes.

Use photos as guides for placement of all pieces. See Tips, page 45.

Attach safety eyes to Rnd 10 spacing them approximately 7 sc apart.

Rnd 20: (Sc2tog, sc in next 4 sc) around: 30 sc.

Rnd 21: (Sc2tog, sc in next 3 sc) around: 24 sc.

Rnd 22: (Sc2tog, sc in next 2 sc) around: 18 sc.

Stuff Body with polyester fiberfill.

Rnd 23: (Sc2tog, sc in next sc) around: 12 sc.

Rnd 24: Sc2tog around: 6 sc.

Continue to sc2tog around until hole is closed; slip st in next sc, finish off.

Eyelid (Make 2)**:** With Gold, ch 4; finish off leaving a long end for sewing.

Sew Eyelids to Body above the safety eyes. Pinch the area between the eyes together to form a bridge and make a couple of stitches from side to side near the inner eyes to hold it in place.

MOUTH

With Gold, ch 10.

Rnd 1 (Right side)**:** Sc in second ch from hook, ch 6, skip next 7 chs, (sc, ch 2, sc) in last ch; working in unworked chs, sc in next 8 chs; do **not** join.

Rnd 2: (Sc, ch 2, sc) in next sc, sc in next 6 chs, slip st in next sc; finish off leaving a long end for sewing.

Use whipstitch *(Fig. 5, page 46)* for the method of sewing to join the pieces together.

Sew Mouth to Rnds 13-15 of Body, centered between safety eyes.

CHEEK (Make 2)

Rnd 1 (Right side)**:** With Gold, make an adjustable loop to form a ring; work 6 sc in ring; do **not** join, place marker.

Rnd 2: 2 Sc in each sc around: 12 sc.

Rnd 3: Sc in each sc around; slip st in next sc, finish off leaving a long end for sewing.

Sew Cheeks to Body on each side of Mouth, stuffing lightly with polyester fiberfill before closing.

FIN (Make 4)

With Gold, ch 4, dc in fourth ch from hook, (ch 1, dc in same ch) twice; finish off leaving a long end for sewing.

Sew 2 Fins to sides of Body and 1 Fin to top and to bottom of Tail.

SPIKES
(Make one each Gold and Aran)

Ch 4, slip st in second ch from hook, sc in next ch, dc in next ch, ★ ch 8, slip st in second ch from hook, sc in next ch, dc in next ch; repeat from ★ 17 times **more**; finish off leaving a long end for sewing.

Sew Spikes to Body.

TAIL

Rnd 1 (Right side)**:** With Gold, make an adjustable loop to form a ring; work 6 sc in ring; do **not** join, place marker.

Rnd 2: 2 Sc in each sc around: 12 sc.

Rnds 3 and 4: Sc in each sc around.

Rnd 5: (Sc in next sc, 2 sc in next sc) around: 18 sc.

Rnd 6: Sc in each sc around; slip st in next sc, finish off leaving a long end for sewing.

Stuff Tail with polyester fiberfill.

Sew Tail to Body.

TAIL FIN

With Gold, ch 5, tr in fifth ch from hook, (ch 1, tr in same ch) twice, ch 5, slip st in same ch; finish off leaving a long end for sewing.

Sew Tail Fin to beginning ring of Tail.

Diagram

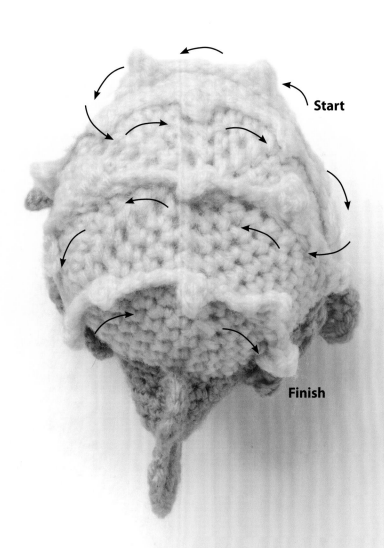

Start

Finish

Finished Size: Approximately 9" (23 cm) tall

MERMAID

HEAD

Rnd 1 (Right side)**:** With Tan, make an adjustable loop to form a ring *(Figs. 1a-d, page 45)*; work 6 sc in ring; do **not** join, place marker to indicate beginning of rnd *(see Markers, page 45).*

Rnd 2: 2 Sc in each sc around: 12 sc.

Rnd 3: (Sc in next sc, 2 sc in next sc) around: 18 sc.

Rnd 4: (Sc in next 2 sc, 2 sc in next sc) around: 24 sc.

Rnd 5: (Sc in next 3 sc, 2 sc in next sc) around: 30 sc.

Rnds 6-11: Sc in each sc around.

The loop can be slipped from the hook onto a safety pin while attaching the eyes.

Use photos as guides for placement of all pieces and for embroidery. See Tips, page 45.

Attach safety eyes to Rnd 6 spacing them approximately 4 sc apart.

Rnd 12: (Sc2tog, sc in next 3 sc) around: 24 sc.

Rnd 13: (Sc2tog, sc in next 2 sc) around: 18 sc.

Stuff Head with polyester fiberfill.

Rnd 14: (Sc2tog, sc in next sc) around: 12 sc.

Rnd 15: Sc2tog around: 6 sc.

Continue to sc2tog around until hole is closed; slip st in next sc, finish off.

CHEEK (Make 2)

Rnd 1 (Right side)**:** With Tan, make an adjustable loop to form a ring; work 6 sc in ring; do **not** join, place marker.

Rnd 2: (Sc in next sc, 2 sc in next sc) around: 9 sc.

Rnd 3: Sc in each sc around; slip st in next sc, finish off leaving a long end for sewing.

NOSE

Rnd 1 (Right side)**:** With Tan, make an adjustable loop to form a ring; work 6 sc in ring; do **not** join, place marker.

Rnd 2: Sc in each sc around; slip st in next sc, finish off leaving a long end for sewing.

EAR (Make 2)

With Tan, ch 2, 5 sc in second ch from hook; finish off leaving a long end for sewing.

FACE

Eyelid (Make 2)**:** With Tan, ch 3; finish off leaving a long end for sewing.

Sew Eyelids to Head above the safety eyes.

Use whipstitch *(Fig. 5, page 46)* for the method of sewing to join the pieces together.

Sew Nose to Rnds 7-9 of Head, stuffing lightly with polyester fiberfill before closing. Sew one Cheek on each side of Nose, just below eyes, stuffing lightly with polyester fiberfill before closing.

Sew Ears to Head.

Pinch the area between the eyes together to form a bridge and make a couple of stitches from side to side near the inner eyes to hold it in place.

With Pink, embroider mouth using backstitch *(Fig. 6, page 46)*. With Black, embroider 2 eyelashes for each eye using straight stitch *(Fig. 7, page 46)*.
With Mint, add a straight stitch over the eyes for the eyebrows.

BODY

Rnd 1 (Right side): With Variegated, make an adjustable loop to form a ring; work 6 sc in ring; do **not** join, place marker.

Rnds 2-4: Sc in each sc around.

Rnd 5: 2 Sc in each sc around: 12 sc.

Rnds 6-8: Sc in each sc around.

Rnd 9: (Sc in next sc, 2 sc in next sc) around: 18 sc.

Rnds 10 and 11: Sc in each sc around.

Rnd 12: (Sc in next 2 sc, 2 sc in next sc) around: 24 sc.

Rnds 13 and 14: Sc in each sc around.

Rnd 15: (Sc in next 3 sc, 2 sc in next sc) around: 30 sc.

Rnds 16 and 17: Sc in each sc around.

Rnd 18: (Sc in next 4 sc, 2 sc in next sc) around: 36 sc.

Rnd 19: Sc in each sc around.

Rnd 20: Sc in each sc around changing to Tan in last sc made *(Fig. 4a, page 46)*.

Rnd 21: Sc in Back Loop Only of each sc around *(Fig. 2, page 45)*.

Rnds 22-25: Sc in both loops of each sc around.

Rnd 26: (Sc2tog, sc in next 4 sc) around: 30 sc.

Rnd 27: Sc in each sc around.

Rnd 28: (Sc2tog, sc in next 3 sc) around: 24 sc.

Rnd 29: Sc in each sc around.

Rnd 30: (Sc2tog, sc in next 2 sc) around; slip st in next sc, finish off leaving a long end for sewing: 18 sc.

Stuff Body with polyester fiberfill.

Sew Body to Head.

FIN
FIRST SIDE

With Variegated, ch 13.

Row 1: Dc in third ch from hook and in next 5 chs, hdc in next 2 chs, sc in next 2 chs, 3 sc in next ch; working in free loops of beginning ch *(Fig. 3b, page 46)*, sc in next 2 chs, hdc in next 2 chs, dc in next 6 chs; do **not** join, finish off.

SECOND SIDE

Work same as First Side, do **not** finish off.

Row 2 (Joining): Ch 1, turn; sc in first 11 sts, 3 sc in next sc, sc in next 11 sts; working on First Side, sc in first 11 sts, 3 sc in next sc, sc in next 11 sts; finish off leaving a long end for sewing.

Sew Fin to bottom of Body.

SHOULDER (Make 2)

Rnd 1 (Right side)**:** With Tan, make an adjustable loop to form a ring; work 6 sc in ring; do **not** join, place marker.

Rnd 2: (Sc in next sc, 2 sc in next sc) around: 9 sc.

Rnds 3 and 4: Sc in each sc around.

Slip st in next sc, finish off leaving a long end for sewing.

Sew Shoulders to Body, stuffing with polyester fiberfill before closing.

ARM (Make 2)

Rnd 1 (Right side)**:** With Tan, make an adjustable loop to form a ring; work 6 sc in ring; do **not** join, place marker.

Rnd 2: (Sc in next sc, 2 sc in next sc) around: 9 sc.

Rnds 3-7: Sc in each sc around.

Slip st in next sc, finish off leaving a long end for sewing.

Stuff Arms with polyester fiberfill.

Sew Arms to Shoulders.

HAND (Make 2)
FINGER (Make 4)

Rnd 1 (Right side)**:** With Tan, make an adjustable loop to form a ring; work 5 sc in ring; do **not** join, place marker.

Rnds 2 and 3: Sc in each sc around.

Finish off first 3 Fingers only.

PALM & BACK

Rnd 1 (Joining rnd)**:** Sc in next 3 sc, sc in any sc on next 2 Fingers, sc in next 3 sc on last Finger; sc in sc on opposite side of next 2 middle Fingers; do **not** join, place marker: 10 sc.

Rnds 2 and 3: Sc in each sc around.

Slip st in next sc, finish off leaving a long end for sewing.

Sew spaces between Fingers closed. Sew Hands to beginning end of Arms, stuffing lightly with polyester fiberfill before closing.

SHELL (Make 2)

Row 1: With Purple, ch 2, 2 sc in second ch from hook.

Row 2: Ch 1, turn; 2 sc in each sc: 4 sc.

Row 3 (Right side)**:** Ch 1, turn; sc in first sc, 2 sc in next sc, sc in next sc, 2 sc in last sc; finish off leaving a long end for sewing: 6 sc.

Sew Shells to Body; with same yarn, embroider straps using backstitch.

FLOWER

With Purple, ch 2, sc in second ch from hook, ch 4, sc in second ch from hook and in next 2 chs, ★ sc in same ch as first sc, ch 4, sc in second ch from hook and in next 2 chs; repeat from ★ 3 times **more**; join with slip st to first sc, finish off leaving a long end for sewing.

HAIR

Cut approximately 75 strands of Mint, each 12" (30.5 cm) long.

Fold one strand in half. Using a crochet hook, draw the folded end up through a stitch on the Head and pull the loose ends through the folded end *(Fig. A)*; draw the knot up tightly. Repeat, spacing strands to cover Head.

Fig. A

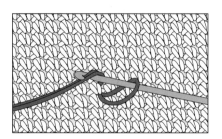

To style the hair, draw a group of the fringe across the forehead to the side of the face and sew the Flower around the group, then tack in place.

Finished Size: Approximately 11" long x 5" high (28 cm x 12.5 cm)

SEAL

HEAD

Rnd 1 (Right side)**:** With White, make an adjustable loop to form a ring *(Figs. 1a-d, page 45)*; work 6 sc in ring; do **not** join, place marker to indicate beginning of rnd *(see Markers, page 45)*.

Rnd 2: 2 Sc in each sc around: 12 sc.

Rnd 3: (Sc in next sc, 2 sc in next sc) around: 18 sc.

Rnd 4: (Sc in next 2 sc, 2 sc in next sc) around: 24 sc.

Rnd 5: (Sc in next 3 sc, 2 sc in next sc) around: 30 sc.

Rnd 6: (Sc in next 4 sc, 2 sc in next sc) around: 36 sc.

Rnd 7: (Sc in next 5 sc, 2 sc in next sc) around: 42 sc.

Rnds 8-15: Sc in each sc around.

The loop can be slipped from the hook onto a safety pin while attaching the eyes.

Use photos as guides for placement of all pieces and for embroidery. See Tips, page 45.

Attach safety eyes to Rnd 3 on each side of center.

Rnd 16: (Sc2tog, sc in next 5 sc) around: 36 sc.

Rnd 17: (Sc2tog, sc in next 4 sc) around: 30 sc.

Rnd 18: (Sc2tog, sc in next 3 sc) around: 24 sc.

Rnd 19: (Sc2tog, sc in next 2 sc) around: 18 sc.

Stuff Head with polyester fiberfill.

Rnd 20: (Sc2tog, sc in next sc) around: 12 sc.

Rnd 21: Sc2tog around: 6 sc.

Continue to sc2tog around until hole is closed; slip st in next sc, finish off.

LOWER JAW

Rnd 1 (Right side)**:** With White, ch 3, 12 dc in third ch from hook; join with slip st to first dc, finish off leaving a long end for sewing.

Note: Loop a short piece of yarn around any dc to mark Rnd 1 as **right** side.

UPPER JAW (Make 2)

Rnd 1 (Right side): With White, ch 3, 8 dc in third ch from hook changing to Light Grey in last dc made *(Fig. 4b, page 46)*, 4 dc in same ch; join with slip st to first dc, finish off leaving a long end for sewing: 12 dc.

Note: Mark Rnd 1 as **right** side.

NOSE

Rnd 1 (Right side): With Black, ch 3, 6 dc in third ch from hook; finish off leaving a long end for sewing.

Note: Mark Rnd 1 as **right** side.

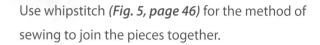

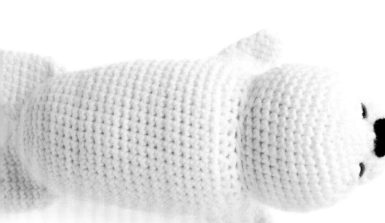

Use whipstitch *(Fig. 5, page 46)* for the method of sewing to join the pieces together.

Sew Lower Jaw to Head. Sew Upper Jaws to Head with Light Grey edges touching, placing them under the safety eyes and overlapping the top edge of the Lower Jaw.

Sew Nose to the Upper Jaws, then embroider a line from the Nose curving along the bottom of the Upper Jaws using backstitch *(Fig. 6, page 46)*.

HEAD ASSEMBLY

Eyelid (Make 2): With White, ch 3; finish off leaving a long end for sewing.

Sew Eyelids to Head above the safety eyes.

Pinch the area between the eyes together to form a bridge; using White, make a couple of stitches from side to side near the inner eyes to hold it in place.

Lightly stuff Lower and Upper Jaws with polyester fiberfill.

BODY

Work same as Head, page 27, through Rnd 6: 36 sc.

Rnds 7-13: Sc in each sc around.

Rnd 14: (Sc in next 5 sc, 2 sc in next sc) around: 42 sc.

Rnds 15-29: Sc in each sc around.

Rnd 30: Sc2tog, (sc in next 2 sc, sc2tog) 5 times, sc in next 20 sc: 36 sc.

Rnd 31: Sc2tog, (sc in next sc, sc2tog) 5 times, sc in next 19 sc; slip st in next sc, finish off leaving a long end for sewing: 30 sc.

Stuff Body with polyester fiberfill.

Place Body over Head at a slight angle and sew in place.

FORELIMB (Make 2)
UPPER LIMB

Rnd 1 (Right side)**:** With White, make an adjustable loop to form a ring; work 6 sc in ring; do **not** join, place marker.

Rnd 2: 2 Sc in each sc around: 12 sc.

Rnd 3: (Sc in next sc, 2 sc in next sc) around: 18 sc.

Rnd 4: Sc in each sc around; slip st in next sc, finish off leaving a long end for sewing.

Stuff Upper Limb with polyester fiberfill.

Sew Upper Limb to Body.

LOWER LIMB

Work same as Upper Limb through Rnd 3: 18 sc.

Rnds 4-6: Sc in each sc around.

Slip st in next sc, finish off leaving a long end for sewing.

Stuff Lower Limb with polyester fiberfill.

Sew Lower Limb to Upper Limb.

FLIPPER

Rnd 1 (Right side)**:** With White, make an adjustable loop to form a ring; work 6 sc in ring; do **not** join, place marker.

Rnd 2: Sc in next 2 sc, 3 sc in next sc, sc in next 3 sc: 8 sc.

Rnd 3: Sc in next 3 sc, 3 sc in next sc, sc in next 4 sc: 10 sc.

Rnd 4: Sc in next 4 sc, 3 sc in next sc, sc in next 5 sc: 12 sc.

Rnd 5: Sc in next 5 sc, 3 sc in next sc, sc in next 6 sc: 14 sc.

Rnd 6: Sc in each sc around; slip st in next sc, finish off leaving a long end for sewing.

Sew Flipper to Lower Limb without stuffing.

HIND FLIPPERS
FLIPPER (Make 2)

Work same as Forelimb Flipper, page 29, through Rnd 5: 14 sc.

Rnd 6: Sc in each sc around.

Rnd 7: Sc in next 6 sc, 3 sc in next sc, sc in next 7 sc: 16 sc.

Rnd 8: Sc in each sc around.

Rnd 9: Sc in next 7 sc, 3 sc in next sc, sc in next 8 sc: 18 sc.

Rnd 10: Sc in next 8 sc, 3 sc in next sc, sc in next 9 sc: 20 sc.

Finish off first Flipper only.

BASE

Rnd 1: Sc in next 9 sc, holding both Flippers together with angled edges facing, sc in third sc of 3-sc group on first Flipper, sc in each sc around leaving one sc on each Flipper unworked: 38 sc.

Rnd 2: Sc2tog, sc in next 15 sc, sc2tog twice, sc in next 15 sc, sc2tog: 34 sc.

Rnd 3: Sc2tog, sc in next 13 sc, sc2tog twice, sc in next 13 sc, sc2tog; slip st in next sc, finish off leaving a long end for sewing: 30 sc.

Sew Base of Hind Flippers to Body without stuffing.

Finished Size: Approximately 12" long x 3½" high (30.5 cm x 9 cm) (excluding Dorsal Fin)

SHARK

BODY

With Grey, ch 4.

Rnd 1 (Right side)**:** Sc in second ch
from hook and in next ch, 3 sc in last
ch; working in free loops of
beginning ch *(Fig. 3b, page 46)*, sc in
next ch, 2 sc in next ch; do **not** join,
place marker to indicate beginning
of rnd *(see Markers, page 45)*: 8 sc.

Rnd 2: (Sc in next 3 sc, 3 sc in next sc)
twice: 12 sc.

Rnd 3: (Sc in next 3 sc, 2 sc in each of
next 3 sc) twice: 18 sc.

Rnd 4: (Sc in next sc, 2 sc in next sc)
around: 27 sc.

Rnds 5 and 6: Sc in each sc around.

Rnd 7: (Sc in next 2 sc, 2 sc in next sc)
around: 36 sc.

Rnd 8: Sc in each sc around.

Rnd 9: (Sc in next 3 sc, 2 sc in next sc)
around: 45 sc.

Rnds 10-29: Sc in each sc around.

The loop can be slipped from
the hook onto a safety pin while
attaching the eyes.

Use photos as guides for placement
of all pieces and for embroidery. See
Tips, page 45.

Holding beginning ch horizontal, attach
safety eyes to each side of Rnd 9.

Rnd 30: (Sc2tog, sc in next 7 sc)
around: 40 sc.

Rnds 31-33: Sc in each sc around.

Rnd 34: (Sc2tog, sc in next 6 sc)
around: 35 sc.

Rnds 35-37: Sc in each sc around.

Rnd 38: (Sc2tog, sc in next 5 sc)
around: 30 sc.

Rnds 39-41: Sc in each sc around.

Rnd 42: (Sc2tog, sc in next 4 sc)
around: 25 sc.

Rnds 43-45: Sc in each sc around.

Rnd 46: (Sc2tog, sc in next 3 sc)
around: 20 sc.

Rnds 47-49: Sc in each sc around.

Rnd 50: (Sc2tog, sc in next 2 sc)
around: 15 sc.

Rnds 51-53: Sc in each sc around.

Stuff Body with polyester fiberfill.

Rnd 54: (Sc2tog, sc in next sc) around: 10 sc.

Rnd 55: Sc2tog around: 5 sc.

Continue to sc2tog around until hole is closed; slip st in next sc, finish off.

Eyelid (Make 2)**:** With Grey, ch 4; finish off leaving a long end for sewing.

Sew Eyelids to Body above the safety eyes.

BELLY

With White, ch 21.

Rnd 1 (Right side)**:** Dc in third ch from hook and in each ch across to last ch, 6 dc in last ch; working in free loops of beginning ch, dc in next 17 chs, 3 dc in next ch, ch 17, sc in second ch from hook and in next 9 chs, hdc in next 4 chs, dc in next 2 chs, 2 dc around post of last dc of 3-dc group; join with slip st to top of beginning ch.

Note: Loop a short piece of yarn around any stitch to mark Rnd 1 as **right** side.

Rnd 2: Ch 3 (**counts as first dc**), dc in next 18 dc, 2 dc in each of next 6 dc, dc in next 20 dc; working in free loops of ch, dc in next 13 chs, 2 dc in each of next 3 chs and in next 3 sc, dc in next 15 sts; join with slip st to first dc: 91 dc.

Rnd 3: Ch 1, sc in same st as joining and in next 3 dc, hdc in next 4 dc, dc in next 8 dc, hdc in next 2 dc, sc in next 2 dc, 2 sc in each of next 10 dc, sc in next 2 dc, hdc in next 2 dc, dc in next 8 dc, hdc in next 4 dc, sc in next 4 dc; slip st in next dc, leave remaining sts unworked, finish off leaving a long end for sewing.

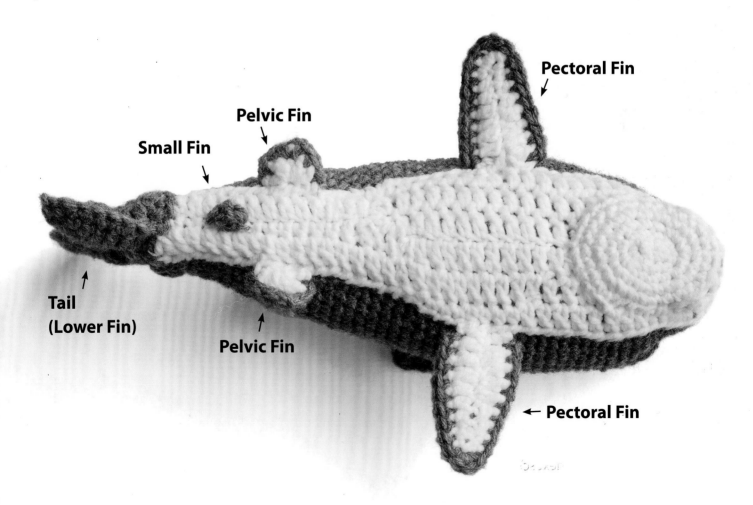

Pectoral Fin

Pelvic Fin

Small Fin

Tail (Lower Fin)

Pelvic Fin

← **Pectoral Fin**

Use whipstitch *(Fig. 5, page 46)* for the method of sewing to join the pieces together.

Placing widest end of Belly at beginning ch of Body, sew in place.

With Grey, embroider nostrils on Rnd 3 of Belly, using a straight stitch for each one *(Fig. 7, page 46)*.

MOUTH
With White, ch 4.

Rnd 1 (Right side)**:** Sc in second ch from hook and in next ch, 3 sc in last ch; working in free loops of beginning ch, sc in next ch, 2 sc in next ch; do **not** join, place marker: 8 sc.

Note: Mark Rnd 1 as **right** side.

Rnd 2: (Sc in next 3 sc, 3 sc in next sc) twice: 12 sc.

Rnd 3: (Sc in next 3 sc, 2 sc in each of next 3 sc) twice: 18 sc.

Rnd 4: (Sc in next sc, 2 sc in next sc) around: 27 sc.

Rnd 5: Sc in each sc around; slip st in next sc, finish off leaving a long end for sewing.

TEETH
Row 1: With White, ch 2, sc in second ch from hook, (ch 3, sc in second ch from hook) 5 times; finish off leaving a long end for sewing.

Row 2: Rotate Row 1 to work in free loops of chs at base of each sc; join Pink with sc in ch at base of last sc made *(see Joining With Sc, page 45)*; (sc around next ch, sc in ch at base of next sc) 5 times; finish off.

Using White, sew Teeth to **wrong** side of Mouth; sew remaining sts on Mouth to Belly.

DORSAL FIN
FIRST SIDE
With Grey, ch 8.

Row 1: Dc in third ch from hook and in next 4 chs, (dc, hdc, ch 2, sc, hdc) in last ch; working in free loops of beginning ch, dc in next 5 chs; do **not** join.

Row 2: Ch 1, turn; sc in first 7 sts, leave remaining sts unworked; finish off.

SECOND SIDE
Work same as First Side.

Joining: Hold both Sides together matching sts; working through **both** layers, join Grey with sc in first dc on Row 1; sc in next 4 dc, 2 sc in each of next 2 sts, (sc, ch 2, sc) in next ch-2 sp, sc in last 7 sc; finish off leaving a long end for sewing.

Beginning on Rnd 23 of Body, sew Dorsal Fin to top of Body.

PECTORAL FIN (Make 2)
LOWER
With White, ch 11.

Row 1 (Right side)**:** Dc in third ch from hook and in next 4 chs, hdc in next 2 chs, sc in next ch, 3 sc in last ch; working in free loops of beginning ch, sc in next ch, hdc in next 2 chs, dc in next 5 chs; do **not** join, finish off: 19 sts.

Note: Mark Row 1 as **right** side.

UPPER
With Grey, work same as Lower Fin; do **not** finish off: 19 sts.

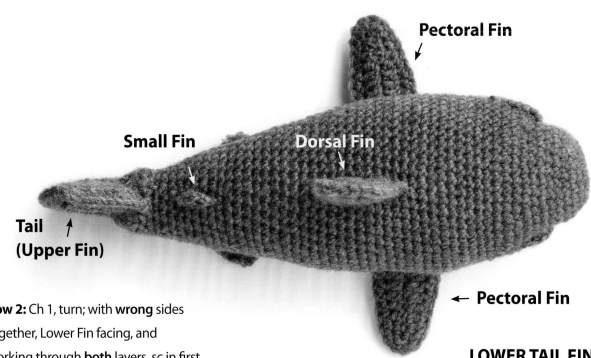

Pectoral Fin

Small Fin

Dorsal Fin

Tail
(Upper Fin)

← **Pectoral Fin**

Row 2: Ch 1, turn; with **wrong** sides together, Lower Fin facing, and working through **both** layers, sc in first 9 sts, 3 sc in next st, sc in next 9 sts; finish off leaving a long end for sewing.

Beginning on Rnd 21 of Body, sew Pectoral Fins to Body at edge of Belly.

PELVIC FIN (Make 2)
LOWER

Row 1 (Right side)**:** With White, ch 3, (dc, ch 2, 2 dc) in third ch from hook; finish off leaving a long end for sewing.

UPPER

Row 1 (Right side)**:** With Grey, ch 3, (dc, ch 2, 2 dc) in third ch from hook.

Row 2: Ch 1, turn; with **wrong** sides together, Lower Fin facing, and working through **both** layers, sc in first 2 dc, (sc, ch 2, sc) in next ch-2 sp, sc in last 2 dc; finish off leaving a long end for sewing.

Skipping 11 rnds from Pectoral Fins, sew Pelvic Fins to Body at edge of Belly.

SMALL FIN (Make 2)

With Grey, ch 3, 2 dc in third ch from hook; finish off leaving a long end for sewing.

Sew one Small Fin to top of Body for the second dorsal fin and one to the Belly for the anal fin.

TAIL
UPPER TAIL FIN
SIDE (Make 2)
With Grey, ch 13.

Rnd 1: 4 Dc in third ch from hook, dc in next 4 chs, hdc in next 3 chs, sc in next 2 chs, (sc, ch 2, sc, hdc) in last ch; working in free loops of beginning ch, dc in next 2 chs, ch 2, dc around post of last dc made, sc in next ch, dc in next 6 chs; join with slip st to first dc, finish off.

LOWER TAIL FIN
SIDE (Make 2)
With Grey, ch 8.

Rnd 1: Dc in third ch from hook and in next 4 chs, (hdc, sc, ch 2, sc, hdc) in last ch; working in free loops of beginning ch, dc in next 4 chs, 5 dc in next ch; join with slip st to first dc, finish off.

JOINING TAIL FINS

Hold Upper Tail Fins together matching sts; working through **both** layers, join Grey with sc in fifth dc; sc in next 9 sts, (sc, ch 2, sc) in next ch-2 sp, sc in next 4 sts, (sc, ch 2, sc) in next ch-2 sp, sc in next dc, skip next sc, sc in next 6 dc, leave remaining sts unworked. Hold Lower Fins together matching sts; working through **both** layers, sc in first 7 sts, (sc, ch 2, sc) in next ch-2 sp, sc in next 7 sts, leave remaining sts unworked; finish off leaving a long end for sewing.

Sew Tail to end of Body.

Finished Size: Approximately 8" (20.5 cm) diameter

BODY

Rnd 1 (Right side)**:** With Variegated,
make an adjustable loop to form a
ring *(Figs. 1a-d, page 45)*; work 6 sc
in ring; do **not** join, place marker to
indicate beginning of rnd *(see
Markers, page 45)*.

Rnd 2: 2 Sc in each sc around: 12 sc.

Rnd 3: (Sc in next sc, 2 sc in next sc)
around: 18 sc.

Rnd 4: (Sc in next 2 sc, 2 sc in next sc)
around: 24 sc.

Rnd 5: (Sc in next 3 sc, 2 sc in next sc)
around: 30 sc.

Rnd 6: (Sc in next 4 sc, 2 sc in next sc)
around: 36 sc.

Rnds 7-13: Sc in each sc around.

The loop can be slipped from
the hook onto a safety pin while
attaching the eyes and embroidering
the mouth.

Use photos as guides for placement
of all pieces and for embroidery. See
Tips, page 45.

Attach safety eyes to Rnd 3 on each
side of center.

With Black, embroider mouth across
top of 6 sc on Rnd 3, using backstitch
(Fig. 6, page 46).

Rnd 14: Working in Back Loops Only
(Fig. 2, page 45), (sc2tog, sc in next
4 sc) around: 30 sc.

Rnd 15: Working in both loops,
(sc2tog, sc in next 3 sc) around: 24 sc.

Rnd 16: (Sc2tog, sc in next 2 sc)
around: 18 sc.

Stuff Body with polyester fiberfill.

Rnd 17: (Sc2tog, sc in next sc)
around: 12 sc.

Rnd 18: Sc2tog around: 6 sc.

Continue to sc2tog around until hole
is closed; slip st in next sc, finish off.

TOP POINT (Make 3)

Rnd 1 (Right side)**:** With Variegated,
make an adjustable loop to form a
ring; work 6 sc in ring; do **not** join,
place marker.

Rnd 2: Sc in each sc around.

Rnd 3: 2 Sc in each of next 3 sc, sc in
next 3 sc: 9 sc.

Rnd 4: Sc in each sc around.

Rnd 5: 2 Sc in next sc, (sc in next sc,
2 sc in next sc) twice, sc in next 4 sc:
12 sc.

37

Rnds 6 and 7: Sc in each sc around.

Rnd 8: (Sc in next sc, 2 sc in next sc) around: 18 sc.

Rnds 9 and 10: Sc in each sc around.

Rnd 11: (Sc in next 2 sc, 2 sc in next sc) around: 24 sc.

Rnds 12-15: Sc in each sc around.

Rnd 16: (Sc in next sc, 2 sc in next sc) around; slip st in next sc, finish off leaving a long end for sewing: 36 sc.

BOTTOM POINT
(Make 2)

Work same as Top Point, page 37, through Rnd 14: 24 sc.

Slip st in next sc, finish off leaving a long end for sewing.

Stuff Top and Bottom Points with polyester fiberfill.

Use whipstitch *(Fig. 5, page 46)* for the method of sewing to join the pieces together.

Pin Points around Body and sew in place.

LARGE DOT (Make 6 with Orchid and 11 with Pink)

Rnd 1 (Right side)**:** Make an adjustable loop to form a ring; work 6 sc in ring; join with slip st to first sc, finish off leaving a long end for sewing.

SMALL DOT (Make 3)

Rnd 1 (Right side)**:** With Orchid, make an adjustable loop to form a ring; work 4 sc in ring; join with slip st to first sc, finish off leaving a long end for sewing.

Sew Dots to Star as desired.

Finished Size: Approximately 10" long x 4" high (25.5 cm x 10 cm)

WHALE

BODY

Rnd 1 (Right side)**:** Make an adjustable loop to form a ring *(Figs. 1a-d, page 45)*; work 6 sc in ring; do **not** join, place marker to indicate beginning of rnd *(see Markers, page 45).*

Rnd 2: 2 Sc in each sc around: 12 sc.

Rnd 3: (Sc in next sc, 2 sc in next sc) around: 18 sc.

Rnd 4: (Sc in next 2 sc, 2 sc in next sc) around: 24 sc.

Rnd 5: (Sc in next 3 sc, 2 sc in next sc) around: 30 sc.

Rnd 6: (Sc in next 4 sc, 2 sc in next sc) around: 36 sc.

Rnds 7-14: Sc in each sc around.

Rnd 15: (Sc in next 5 sc, 2 sc in next sc) around: 42 sc.

The loop can be slipped from the hook onto a safety pin while attaching the eyes.

Use photos as guides for placement of all pieces. See Tips, page 45.

Attach safety eyes to Rnd 10 on each side.

Rnd 16: Sc in each sc around.

Rnd 17: (Sc in next 6 sc, 2 sc in next sc) around: 48 sc.

Rnds 18-33: Sc in each sc around.

Rnd 34: (Sc2tog, sc in next 6 sc) around: 42 sc.

Rnds 35 and 36: Sc in each sc around.

Rnd 37: (Sc2tog, sc in next 5 sc) around: 36 sc.

Rnd 38: Sc in each sc around.

Rnd 39: (Sc2tog, sc in next 4 sc) around: 30 sc.

Rnd 40: (Sc2tog, sc in next 3 sc) around: 24 sc.

Rnd 41: (Sc2tog, sc in next 2 sc) around: 18 sc.

Stuff Body with polyester fiberfill.

Rnd 42: (Sc2tog, sc in next sc) around: 12 sc.

Rnd 43: Sc2tog around: 6 sc.

Continue to sc2tog around until hole is closed; slip st in next sc, finish off.

Eyelid (Make 2)**:** Ch 3; finish off leaving a long end for sewing.

Sew Eyelids to Head above the safety eyes.

MOUTH

Row 1: Ch 3, 6 dc in third ch from hook **(2 skipped chs count as first dc):** 7 dc.

Row 2 (Right side)**:** Ch 3 **(counts as first dc, now and throughout)**, turn; dc in first dc, 2 dc in each of next 6 dc: 14 dc.

Note: Loop a short piece of yarn around any dc to mark Row 2 as **right** side.

Row 3: Ch 3, turn; 2 dc in next dc, (dc in next dc, 2 dc in next dc) across: 21 dc.

Row 4: Ch 3, turn; 5 dc in first dc, skip next 2 dc, sc in next 3 dc, sc in Front Loop Only of next 9 dc *(Fig. 2, page 45)*, sc in **both** loops of next 3 dc, skip next 2 dc, 6 dc in last dc; finish off leaving a long end for sewing: 27 sts.

Use whipstitch *(Fig. 5, page 46)* for the method of sewing to join the pieces together.

Sew Mouth to Body, placing end of Rows 1-3 across Rnd 14 with ends of Row 4 curved down.

TAIL

BASE

Rnd 1 (Right side)**:** Make an adjustable loop to form a ring; work 6 sc in ring; do **not** join, place marker.

Rnd 2: 2 Sc in each sc around: 12 sc.

Rnd 3: (Sc in next sc, 2 sc in next sc) around: 18 sc.

Rnd 4: (Sc in next 2 sc, 2 sc in next sc) around: 24 sc.

Rnd 5: Sc in each sc around.

Rnd 6: (Sc in next 3 sc, 2 sc in next sc) around: 30 sc.

Rnd 7: Sc in each sc around; slip st in next sc, finish off leaving a long end for sewing.

Stuff Base with polyester fiberfill. Sew Base to end of Body.

MIDDLE

Work same as Base, page 41, through Rnd 3: 18 sc.

Rnd 4: Sc in each sc around.

Rnd 5: (Sc in next 2 sc, 2 sc in next sc) around: 24 sc.

Rnd 6: Sc in each sc around; slip st in next sc, finish off leaving a long end for sewing.

Stuff Middle with polyester fiberfill. Sew Middle to Base.

END

Work same as Base, page 41, through Rnd 2: 12 sc.

Rnd 3: Sc in each sc around.

Rnd 4: (Sc in next sc, 2 sc in next sc) around: 18 sc.

Rnd 5: Sc in each sc around; slip st in next sc, finish off leaving a long end for sewing.

Stuff End with polyester fiberfill. Sew End to Middle.

FLUKE BASE

Rnd 1 (Right side)**:** Make an adjustable loop to form a ring; work 6 sc in ring; do **not** join, place marker.

Rnds 2 and 3: Sc in each sc around.

Rnd 4: (Sc in next sc, 2 sc in next sc) around: 9 sc.

Rnds 5 and 6: Sc in each sc around.

Slip st in next sc, finish off leaving a long end for sewing.

Stuff Fluke Base with polyester fiberfill. Sew Fluke Base to End.

RIGHT FLUKE

Rnd 1: Make an adjustable loop to form a ring; ch 2, work 5 dc in ring, ch 3, sc in second ch from hook, dc in next ch and around post of last dc of 5-dc group, 3 sc in ring; join with slip st to top of ch-2.

Rnd 2 (Right side): Ch 1, sc in same st as joining and in next 2 dc, 2 sc in next dc, sc in next 2 dc and in free loop of next 2 chs (*Fig. 3b, page 46*), (sc, ch 2, sc) in ch at tip, sc in next 3 sts, 2 sc in next sc, sc in last 2 sc; join with slip st to first sc, finish off leaving a long end for sewing.

LEFT FLUKE

Rnd 1: Make an adjustable loop to form a ring; ch 2, work 5 dc in ring, ch 3, sc in second ch from hook, dc in next ch and around post of last dc of 5-dc group, 3 sc in ring; join with slip st to top of ch-2.

Rnd 2 (Right side): Ch 1, **turn**; sc in same st as joining and in next 2 sc, 2 sc in next sc, sc in next 3 sts, (sc, ch 2, sc) in ch at tip, sc in free loop of next 2 chs and in next 2 dc, 2 sc in next dc, sc in last 2 dc; join with slip st to first sc, finish off leaving a long end for sewing.

Sew Right and Left Flukes to end of Fluke Base.

FLIPPERS

Work same as Left and Right Flukes of Tail.

Sew a Flipper to each side of Body.

GENERAL INSTRUCTIONS

ABBREVIATIONS

ch(s)	chain(s)
cm	centimeters
dc	double crochet(s)
hdc	half double crochet(s)
mm	millimeters
Rnd(s)	Round(s)
sc	single crochet(s)
sc2tog	single crochet 2 together
sp(s)	space(s)
st(s)	stitch(es)
tr	treble crochet(s)
YO	yarn over

SYMBOLS & TERMS

★ — work instructions following ★ as many **more** times as indicated in addition to the first time.

( ) or [ ] — work enclosed instructions **as many** times as specified by the number immediately following **or** work all enclosed instructions in the stitch or space indicated **or** contains explanatory remarks.

colon (:) — the number(s) given after a colon at the end of a row or round denote(s) the number of stitches or spaces you should have on that row or round.

GAUGE

Gauge is not of great importance; your project may be a little larger or smaller without changing the overall effect. Be sure your crochet fabric is dense enough so that stuffing does not show through your stitches. Use the size hook needed to achieve a tight gauge.

CROCHET TERMINOLOGY	
UNITED STATES	INTERNATIONAL
slip stitch (slip st) =	single crochet (sc)
single crochet (sc) =	double crochet (dc)
half double crochet (hdc) =	half treble crochet (htr)
double crochet (dc) =	treble crochet (tr)
treble crochet (tr) =	double treble crochet (dtr)
double treble crochet (dtr) =	triple treble crochet (ttr)
triple treble crochet (tr tr) =	quadruple treble crochet (qtr)
skip =	miss

Yarn Weight Symbol & Names	LACE 0	SUPER FINE 1	FINE 2	LIGHT 3	MEDIUM 4	BULKY 5	SUPER BULKY 6	JUMBO 7
Type of Yarns in Category	Fingering, size 10 crochet thread	Sock, Fingering, Baby	Sport, Baby	DK, Light Worsted	Worsted, Afghan, Aran	Chunky, Craft, Rug	Super Bulky, Roving	Jumbo, Roving
Crochet Gauge* Ranges in Single Crochet to 4" (10 cm)	32-42 sts**	21-32 sts	16-20 sts	12-17 sts	11-14 sts	8-11 sts	6-9 sts	5 sts and fewer
Advised Hook Size Range	Steel*** 6 to 8, Regular hook B-1	B-1 to E-4	E-4 to 7	7 to I-9	I-9 to K-10½	K-10½ to M/N-13	M/N-13 to Q	Q and larger

*GUIDELINES ONLY: The chart above reflects the most commonly used gauges and hook sizes for specific yarn categories.

CROCHET HOOKS																
U.S.	B-1	C-2	D-3	E-4	F-5	G-6	7	H-8	I-9	J-10	K-10½	L-11	M/N-13	N/P-15	P/Q	Q	S
Metric - mm	2.25	2.75	3.25	3.5	3.75	4	4.5	5	5.5	6	6.5	8	9	10	15	16	19

■□□□ BEGINNER		Projects for first-time crocheters using basic stitches. Minimal shaping.
■■□□ EASY		Projects using yarn with basic stitches, repetitive stitch patterns, simple color changes, and simple shaping and finishing.
■■■□ INTERMEDIATE		Projects using a variety of techniques, such as basic lace patterns or color patterns, mid-level shaping and finishing.
■■■■ EXPERIENCED		Projects with intricate stitch patterns, techniques and dimension, such as non-repeating patterns, multi-color techniques, fine threads, small hooks, detailed shaping and refined finishing.

ADJUSTABLE LOOP

Wind the yarn around two fingers to form a ring (*Fig. 1a*), slide the yarn off your fingers and grasp the strands at the top of the ring (*Fig. 1b*). Insert the hook from **front** to **back** into the ring, pull up a loop, YO and draw through the loop on hook to lock the ring (*Fig. 1c*).

Working around **both** strands, work stitches in the ring as specified, then pull the yarn end to close (*Fig. 1d*).

Fig. 1a

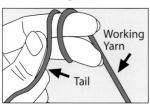

Fig. 1b

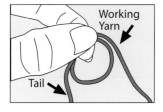

Fig. 1c

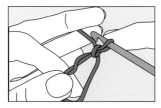

Fig. 1d

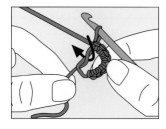

TIPS

SAFETY

If the item is for a child that is at risk of choking, do **not** use beads or buttons as a substitute for the safety eyes. When using safety eyes, it is important to make sure the eyes are attached correctly by following the directions on the package. Make sure that they can't work their way through the crocheted stitches. When in doubt, embroider the Eyes instead (*see Embroidery Stitches, page 46*).

STUFFING

Add plenty of polyester fiberfill to the crocheted pieces to maintain the shape, but not so much that it will show through your stitches.

YARN ENDS

Instead of weaving in yarn ends, they can be inserted into the center of the stuffed parts. Make sure that the yarn used for embroidery is inserted in the center of the piece and doesn't show.

MARKERS

Markers are used to help distinguish the beginning of each round being worked. Place a 2" (5 cm) scrap piece of yarn before the first stitch of each round, moving the marker after each round is complete.

JOINING WITH SC

When instructed to join with sc, begin with a slip knot on hook. Insert hook in stitch or space indicated, YO and pull up a loop, YO and draw through both loops on hook.

BACK OR FRONT LOOP ONLY

Work only in loop(s) indicated by arrow (*Fig. 2*).

Fig. 2

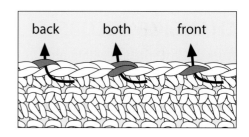

FREE LOOPS

After working in Back or Front Loops Only on a row or round, there will be a ridge of unused loops. These are called the free loops. Later, when instructed to work in the free loops of the same row or round, work in these loops (*Fig. 3a*).

Fig. 3a

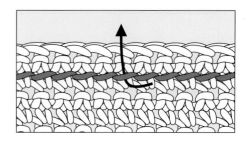

When instructed to work in free loops of a chain, work in loop indicated by arrow *(Fig. 3b)*.

Fig. 3b

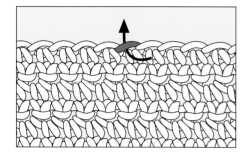

CHANGING COLORS

Work the last stitch to within one step of completion (2 loops on hook), drop yarn, hook new yarn *(Figs. 4a & b)* and draw through both loops on hook. Do **not** cut yarn until indicated.

Fig. 4a

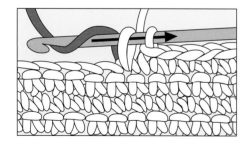

Fig. 4b

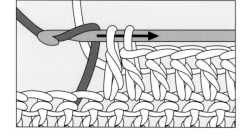

WHIPSTITCH

To sew a piece to another, insert the needle from **front** to **back** through two strands of a stitch **or** through end of a row on the top piece, then through a stitch on the bottom piece *(Fig. 5)*. Bring the needle around and insert it through the next strands on the piece, then through a stitch. Continue working in same manner.

Fig. 5

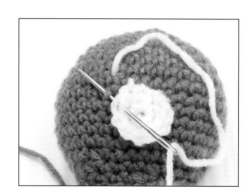

EMBROIDERY STITCHES
BACKSTITCH

Backstitch is worked from right to left. Come up at 1, go down at 2 and come up at 3 *(Fig. 6)*. The second stitch is made by going down at 1 and coming up at 4.

Fig. 6

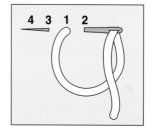

STRAIGHT STITCH

Straight stitch is just what the name implies, a single, straight stitch. Come up at 1 and go down at 2 *(Fig. 7)*.

Fig. 7

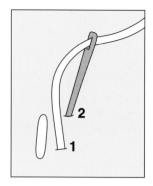

SATIN STITCH

Satin stitch is a series of straight stitches worked side-by-side that touch but do not overlap *(Fig. 8)*. Come up at odd numbers and go down at even numbers.

Fig. 8

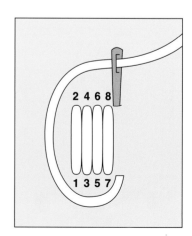

Meet the Designer:

JESSICA BOYER

Jessica Boyer learned to crochet in childhood, taught by her grandmother, but she started crocheting more after she was diagnosed with fibromyalgia in her early twenties. "I like to make amigurumi animals that look semi-realistic and playful," she said. "This is definitely a passion for me, from sketching to crocheting to assembling the pieces."

High school sculptural work and college classes in graphic design have come in handy, she says. "I always work the amigurumi pieces more as I would a soft sculpture. I sketch some quick ideas of what I want the subject to look like, and then I look at as many photos as I possibly can of what I want to make and at every angle possible."

A stay-at-home mom, Jessica loves "cheesy" horror movies, reading, and '90s alternative music. Other arts and crafts that she enjoys are cross stitch, wire jewelry making, and acrylic painting. More of her designs may be found in *Spirit Animals* (Leisure Arts Book #6458), *Home Team Gear* (#6695), *Enchanted Forest Creatures* (#6851), and *Farm Animals* (#75429). Also on Ravelry and Etsy, she blogs at jessboyercrochet.tumblr.com.

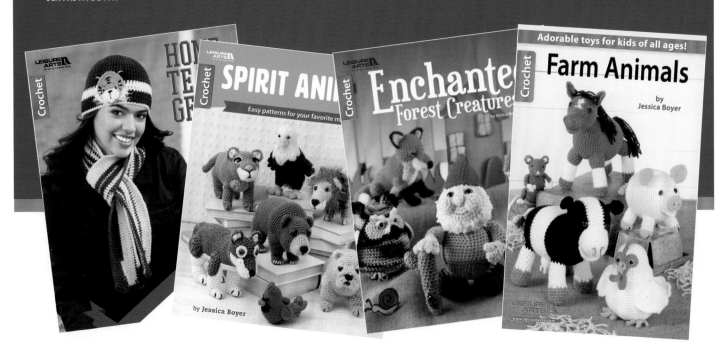

YARN INFORMATION

Each item in this book was made with Red Heart® Super Saver®. Any brand of Medium Weight Yarn may be used. It is best to refer to the yardage/meters when determining how many balls or skeins to purchase. Remember, to arrive at the finished size, it is the GAUGE/TENSION that is important, not the brand of yarn.

For your convenience, listed below are the colors used to create our photography models. Because yarn manufacturers make frequent changes in their product lines, you may sometimes find it necessary to use a substitute yarn or to search for the discontinued product at alternate suppliers (locally or online).

CRAB

Red - #319 Cherry Red

Tan - #334 Buff

Black - #312 Black

SEAHORSE

Yellow - #324 Bright Yellow

Gold - #321 Gold

OCTOPUS

Dark Orange - #256 Carrot

Orange - #254 Pumpkin

Black - #312 Black

PUFFER FISH

Gold - #321 Gold

Aran - #313 Aran

MERMAID

Tan - #334 Buff

Variegated - #3944 Macaw

Mint - #520 Minty

Purple - #528 Medium Purple

Black - #312 Black

Pink - # 706 Perfect Pink

SEAL

White - #311 White

Light Grey - #341 Light Grey

Black - #312 Black

SHARK

Grey - #400 Grey Heather

White - #311 White

Pink - #706 Perfect Pink

STARFISH

Variegated - #940 Plum Pudding

Orchid - #776 Dark Orchid

Pink - #706 Perfect Pink

Black - #312 Black

WHALE

#3933 Dove

Production Team: Instructional/Technical Editor - Cathy Hardy; Editorial Writer - Susan Frantz Wiles; Senior Graphic Artist - Lora Puls; Artist - Kellie McAnulty; Photo Stylist - Lori Wenger; and Photographer - Jason Masters.